Cover designed by Wang Daozhong
Photographs by Jiang Jingyu, Yan Zhongyi, Lu Sicong,
Meng Zhaoyi, Li Chengyong, Zhang Songquan, Yi Mu,
Zhang Jingbao, Mao Zongguo
Editeds by Wang Yanrong, Yu Shenquan .

ISBN 7 − 5054 − 0418 − 0/ J · 0138
84E − 635   04800

Publisher:

Morning Glory Press
(A Subsidiary of China International Book Trading Corporation)
No. 35 Chegongzhuang Xilu, Beijing 100044, China

Distributor:

China International Book Trading Corporation
(Guoji Shudian)
No. 35 Chegongzhuang Xilu , Beijin 100044, China
P.O.Box 399, Beijing

CHINA'S
RARE FLOWERS

Painted in traditional Chinese style by Wu Guoting

Text by Wang Jiaxi and Ma Yue
Translated by Deng Xin

Morning Glory Press
Beijing, 1995

First Edition 1986
Reprinted 1988
Third 1995

Art and Flowers
(An Introduction)

Ma Hongzeng, deputy director of the
Jiangsu Provincial Art Gallery

Flowers, universally loved, beautify life and the environment.

The kingdom of flowers includes many rare species growing all over the world — the common cineraria in Africa, the tulip in southern Europe, the sunflower in America, the cherry in Japan....

This album features 34 illustrations of China's precious flowers. Working with the traditional "gifted brush," Wu Guoting creates a blooming garden on every page. Buds quietly open amid fresh emerald leaves — some are bright and gaudy, some delicate, some coy and others dignified. In a riot of colors, the blooms seem to smile at you, murmur to you and sweetly scent the air around you.

In order to vividly portray each flower, the artist combines the graphic touches, bold outlines and expressive inks of Chinese painting with the Western school's realistic backgrounds and emphasis on light and shade. Set against variable backgrounds, the flowers, leaves and stems interact in lifelike poses. The rich colors and natural grace lure the reader into scenes like the following.

The chrysanthemum has been cultivated in China for 3,000 years. Blossoming in the fall, it is also known as the "gentleman of the flowers," since "it is not as pretty and coquettish as the plum and the peach, but stands erect as the pine and the cypress." Now more than 1,000 varieties exist. Some bloom in clusters of golden yellow flowers; some grow petals that are red inside and golden outside like the rising sun; some have flowers of fluffy curls like a woman's hair. The yellow chrysanthemum pictured in this album is the most ancient species Forceful lines delineate the yellow petals set off by dark leaves, evoking images of flying dragons and dancing phoenixes.

The tree peony, the "king of flowers," symbolizes happiness and good luck. Transparent hues and contrasting colors portray the sparkling, elegant petals. Poet Sima Guang of the Song Dynasty wrote 900 years ago, "Prosperous air reigns Luoyang in spring, with thousands of houses tucked away in the shade of red and green; don't match flowers to embroideries, but match embroideries to flowers." All the traditional flower fairs, flower feasts and flower dances feature tree peonies.

One of the three famous Chinese wild flowers, the primrose blossoms in spring in clusters of small flowers. In the painting, a primrose in the wilderness displays dazzling rose-colored flowers. The traditional seal enhances the painting's meaning. The seven Chinese characters read, "Fragrant grass is to be found everywhere."

Wu Guoting's art captures a heavy bunch of purplish flowers of the Chinese redbud shrub clinging to a twig like exploding fireworks or butterflies fluttering in the air.

The fragrant plantain lily decorates classical Chinese gardens. Contrasting broad dark leaves and stands of bamboo in black ink emphasizes the whiteness of the buds swaying in the wind.

The artist's brush avoids monotony in search of variety. For instance, the stems of the Chinese trumpet creeper mimic the forceful lines of Chinese calligraphy. The Arabian jasmine appears in a pot. A lively butterfly accents the common orange day lily. The lily is set against gurgling springs. A hushed moonlit night envelops the winter sweet. The polyanthus narcissus grows luxuriantly like a forest of swords.

This album brings a panorama of famous Chinese flowers to the armchair traveller.

Human creativity has influenced the history of flowers. The tree peony was a wild low tree when first found in the Taihang Mountains. The narcissus was born in the marshes of southeast China. The wild chrysanthemum grows flowers only the size of a small coin, and the cockscomb used to be as ugly as the green bristle grass. However, through meticulous cultivation and breeding, they all developed into beautiful flowers.

For this portfolio, Wu Guoting, like the horticulturists, has artistically transformed the beauty of nature.

China's Rare Flowers

Mei *Plum* 梅花

(Prunus mume)

Native to China, the plum blossoms in late winter and early spring. For centuries, the plum has symbolized purity and nobility in Chinese literature and art.

This deciduous tree grows up to 10 meters tall with a hard trunk covered with purplish brown or dark brown mottled bark. The red, pink or white flowers sharply contrast the tough branches. On silvery moonlit nights, the tree's slant shadows and faint aroma create a dreamland.

The plum was cultivated in China 3,000 years ago. It likes good sunshine but can stand severe cold. Wild plum trees grow in eastern Sichuan and western Hubei provinces, but the trees are now planted all over the country.

A plum tree can live up to one thousand years, growing more beautiful each year. Planted together with the pine and the bamboo in south China's courtyards, it adds beauty to the winter scene.

Discovered in China, the plum belongs to the rose family. Pink or white flowers bloom between February and March, followed by oval, sharply-toothed leaves.

Winter Jasmine 迎春

(Jasminum nudiflorum)

The north China winter lasts long and spring comes late. The winter jasmine's naked branches are dreary, until clusters of dazzling yellow flowers suddenly appear on dry grey stems. The blooms are harbingers of spring, brightening the bleak world.

A central and northern China shrub, the winter jasmine grows on slopes and precipices. Its spreading stems form a golden screen when the small yellow flowers burst into bloom. Potted winter jasmine can be shaped into many forms.

The winter jasmine, a deciduous shrub, is a member of the olive family. Fine hairs cover the egg-shaped leaves. The yellow flowers bloom from February to April.

Paper Bush 结香

(Edgeworthia chrysantha)

Grown south of the Changjiang River, and also in Henan, Shaanxi and southwestern regions, the paper bush now flourishes widely in Chinese gardens.

In early March, its fragrant flowers herald spring. Profuse leaves sprout after the flowers fall. The flexible stem can be bent to form beautiful shapes, so the paper bush is often planted in pots or gardens together with evergreen shrubs.

The stem and bark are made into paper and rayon. The whole plant is useful in Chinese medicine, while the stem and leaves can be converted into insecticide.

Of the daphne family, the deciduous pap bush, with needlelike, oblong leaves, can rea one meter tall. The fragrant yellow flowers a arranged in hanging capitula.

Peach 桃花

(Prunus persica)

A common image in ancient Chinese poems, the peach was first mentioned in the *Book of Songs* 3,000 years ago: "Its beauty shines with all its brightness." The great poet Su Dongpo of the Song Dynasty wrote these famous lines: "Peach blossoms peep out from behind bamboo groves; ducks float down on the warm spring water."

The fragrant peach flowers in March and April, clothing the whole tree in red. The scarlet peach flowers mixed with green willow leaves compose a typical south China landscape.

Chinese folklores use peach flowers for good luck and happiness, while its fruit symbolizes longevity.

The peach's embryonic fruit and bark can be used as medicine, and its gum is good for making glue.

A member of the rose family, the pea boasts many varieties. It is native to northe and central China, but is now cultivated all ov the country. The peach tree usually grows four or five meters under cultivation. The leav are lance-shaped with single flowers a roundish fruits.

16

Chinese Redbud 紫荆

(Cercis chinensis)

The flower of the Chinese redbud resembles a fluttering butterfly.

The early spring shrub grows wild in western Hubei Province and has been widely planted in North China. The greyish smooth bark of the young redbud cracks as the trunk matures. It likes sunshine, but tolerates cold weather, and flourishes on rich loose soil at high altitudes. The Chinese redbud decorates parks and courtyards.

Before leaves appear, the upturned red or purple petals evoke flying butterflies. The Chinese redbud is sometimes planted with the yellow flowering kerria, enhancing the beauty of both plants.

The bark, pedicel and seed have medicinal value. The seed can also be used in insecticide.

*The deciduous Chinese redbud bush belongs to the pulse family. The alternate round leaves follow the flowers which bloom in **March** and April. The purplish pods, flat and elongated, ripen in September and October.*

18

Lilac Daphne 芫花

(Daphne genkwa)

Originating in China, the lilac daphne grows along the Changjiang River and in Shandong, Henan and Shaanxi provinces. This wild ornamental species resembles the clove but grows much shorter, between half a meter and one meter. The lilac daphne's long-lasting flowers subtly perfume the air.

The lilac daphne grows in parks and courtyards, and along roads. Cut flowers stay fresh up to 20 days.

The bark's soft yet tough tissue provides good industrial material. The flower, bark and root are medicinal ingredients, while the whole plant can be used for making insecticide.

This deciduous shrub belongs to the daphne family. The oblong leaves are generally opposite, but a small number are alternate. Small clusters of light purple or light purplish red flowers open at the leaf axils during March and April.

Azalea 杜鹃

(Rhododendron simsii)

The azalea, primrose and gentian are known in China as the "three famous flowers." The azalea blankets slopes in red, purple, yellow or white in early April. And the cuckoo, attracted to the blooming azalea, comes and sings its sad song.

Since ancient times, the Chinese have called the azalea and cuckoo brother and sister. Tang Dynasty poet Bai Juyi wrote: "In March the cuckoo comes to Jiujiang. It sings and sets the azalea abloom."

Two scarlet lines mark the corners of the cuckoo's beak. According to a Chinese legend, the cuckoo spits blood as it sings to dye the red azalea and hasten spring.

The azalea grows on mountains, in ravines and near forests, and does well in cool, humid weather. Six hundred varieties are native to China, out of 800 world varieties.

A member of the heath family, the azalea is an evergreen or semievergreen shrub. The egg-shaped leaves grow singly and alternately around a funnel-shaped flower

Common Flowering Quince 贴梗海棠

(Chaenomeles lagenaria)

The common flowering quince's short-stemmed, bright red flowers look like those of the Chinese flowering crab apple. The small double blooms with multiple calyxes cluster together. In March, the buds complement the wafting willow catkins and the flowering winter jasmine.

The common flowering quince, a deciduous bush, grows to two meters tall. The erect stems, wrapped in purplish black bark, stand in thick groups. Highly adaptable, it resists cold but is sensitive to light. Consequently, plants growing in shade blossom several days later than those in full sun.

The common flowering quince has spread from China's southwestern regions to places all over the country. It is planted in courtyards, by lakes or roadsides, or formed into hedges. The root and fruit possess medicinal properties.

The common flowering quince belongs to the rose family and has egg-shaped to oblong leaves. The flowers, red, pink or milky white, come in March and April. The rounded sweet-smelling fruit ripens in October.

Primrose 报春花

(Primula)

The primrose bursts into bloom with the first spring breeze. Shaped like miniature umbrellas, the red, pink, purple, blue, white or yellow flowers are covered with fine hair, and contain a poisonous fluid which can cause a skin allergy.

Native to China's Guizhou and Yunnan provinces, the primrose is an annual herb that grows in the wild and by farm fields. It is one of the "three famous Chinese flowers."

An annual herb, the primrose blooms mainly in red, pink or white. The fleshy, stalked leaves may be long and narrow, or roundish.

Yulan Magnolia 玉兰

(Magnolia denudate)

Hanging from high branches, the white yulan magnolia flowers appear in early spring.

Towering up to 15 meters, a flowering yulan dazzles the eye with hundreds of white cups nestled in greenery.

Instead of bending their heads, people gaze up to admire the yulan flowers set against the azure sky.

The fleshy, edible yulan petals smell like orchids and are used in perfume. The bark and buds can be used for making medicine.

A deciduous woody plant, the yulan magnolia originated in China. Belonging to the magnolia family, it has short, round alternate leaves.

Tree Peony 牡丹

(Paeonia suffruticosa)

The elegant tree peony, glorious on a bright spring day, is the king of Chinese flowers. The peony flowers are red, white, purple, yellow, black or green.

The tree peony grows in northern and western China and was domesticated long ago. For centuries it has been known as the "most beautiful of the beauties."

Far back in the seventh century during the Tang Dynasty, residents of the capital city Chang'an (now Xi'an) flocked to buy peonies during the 20-day flowering period. By the Song Dynasty (10th century), the breeding of new varieties was fashionable, and rich people would pay 1,000 pieces of gold for a rare species. The craze for the tree peony continued till the 14th century during the Ming Dynasty.

Now popular ornamental plants, more than 300 tree peony varieties flourish all over China.

Medicines can be made from the root and bark.

The tree peony, a deciduous shrub, belongs to the buttercup family. The feathered compound leaves grow alternately. The flower, single or double, comes in late April and mid-May.

Cymbidium　兰花

(Cymbidium)

Native to China's Zhejiang, Anhui, Henan, Gansu, Sichuan and Yunnan provinces, the cymbidium, a genus of Asian orchids, is a popular ornamental plant. Cultivated for centuries, it is known as the "gentleman of the flowers." The Chinese cymbidium blooms in spring with elegantly fragrant flowers.

The cymbidium is a favorite house plant and blends well with winter jasmine in courtyards.

A nonwoody perennial plant, the cymbidium belongs to the orchid family. The milky white root is pulpy, and the smooth green leaves grow long and narrow with pointed tips. The pale green or pale yellowish green flowers bloom singly or in racemes.

Dove Tree   珙桐

(Davidia involucrata)

Native to China's western Hubei, Sichuan, Guizhou and northern Yunnan provinces, dove trees grow on mountains at 700-2,000 meters above sea level, mostly on the mist-shrouded shady side.

Unique dove-like flowers cover the tree in April and May. Each flower head is framed by two large creamy bracts like the wings of a dove.

Found naturally only in China, the dove tree is prized as an ornamental tree the world over. It survived the Ice Age when some parts of China escaped the destructive glaciers.

The dove tree, constituting the family Davidiaceae, is a deciduous woody plant growing to 15-20 meters, with wide, oval, papery leaves alternately arranged. The terminal flower head consists of a bisexual flower and several male flowers, set off by two large, round or oval, bracts.

歳在甲
子三月
圉子寫

Chinese Rose 月季

(Rosa chinensis)

China produced a great variety of roses 300 years ago. This precious flowering plant spread to Europe in 1789 and immediately became popular. More species were developed there. The Chinese rose, now a world favorite, is known as the queen of flowers.

The flowers, lasting from April to December, appear in white, yellow, red, orange and compound colors; a few are blue and green. The plant appears in erect, trailing or miniature forms.

The large, beautiful flowers often fringe lawns or flower beds. In China, many parks and botanical gardens feature roses.

A member of the rose family, the Chinese rose is a deciduous or semievergreen shrub or vine with prickly stems. The oval leaves grow alternately. The flowers are classified as single, double or semidouble.

Chinese Pink　石竹

(Dianthus chinensis)

A famous ornamental, the Chinese pink, with moss-like green leaves and erect stems, has long been cultivated. It blossoms in May and June with colorful, velvet-rimmed petals.

The Chinese pink is usually planted beside rockeries, in lawns and along roads. It also enhances potted miniature landscapes.

The root, stem, leaves and flowers can be used in Chinese medicine.

The Chinese pink, a perennial herb, is a member of the pink family. The lancelike leaves are opposite and elongated. The flowers, in bright red, pink or white, bloom singly or in small clusters.

38

Lily 百合

(Lilium)

The lily is a native plant of China's Taiwan Province, though it can also be found in Japan. Many varieties have been cultivated since ancient times. Emperor Xuandi of the Later Liang Dynasty praised the lily's charm 1,400 years ago: "Hanging glossy leaves and unusually colored flowers, moistened by the morning dew, sway in the gentle breeze." Many fine species were developed 300 years later, during the Tang Dynasty.

The tall and graceful lily features large, white, elegant flowers, representing purity, brightness, freedom and happiness.

The edible white bulbs are of medical importance.

A species of the lily family, the lily, flowering in May, June and July, is a perennial bulb herb with upright stems. The lanceolate leaves cluster around the stem. The flower head contains several to a dozen creamy flowers.

Hollyhock　蜀葵

(Althaea rosea)

A native plant of China, the hollyhock was first discovered in Sichuan Province. Multiple blossoms in red, white, yellow, purple or black cover the stems to form colorful patterns. Oddly, the flowers of the next generation of hollyhock differ in color from the parent plants.

The hollyhock grows two meters tall. Commonly planted in flower beds, gardens and hedgerows, it has a long flowering period and is highly adaptable.

The flower and seed are made into drugs, while the bark produces fibers for the textile industry.

*The perennial herb hollyhock, of the mal-low family, has large alternate leaves and oval stipules. Blooming from **May** to July, the large and colorful flowers are borne at the axils singly or in clusters of two and three.*

Common Orange Day Lily 萱草

(Hemerocallis fulva)

When the earth steams under the summer sun, the trumpet-shaped red, yellow or white flowers of the common orange day lily stand proudly, visited by butterflies.

Ornamenting courtyards for centuries, the common orange day lily, native to China's Changjiang River valley, can also be planted in flower beds, lawns and rock gardens.

More than 100 varieties of common orange day lily bloom in June and July. Each flower lasts for only one day, hence the name day lily.

The root has sedative and diuretic powers.

A member of the lily family, this perennial flowering plant produces conical flowers arranged in cymose order.

Common Hydrangea　　八仙花

(Hydrangea macrophylla)

A summer ornamental, the common hydrangea features showy flower clusters. Each flower contains one peduncle and eight pistils.

The common hydrangea prospers in a damp, temperate climate, and is cultivated near water or beneath evergreen trees. It is mostly planted in pots which can be moved inside to beautify and freshen rooms.

When dried, the petals effectively treat heatstroke and malaria.

Included in the hydrangea family, the common hydrangea, a deciduous shrub, has large, oval, opposite leaves. The globular clusters of flowers, in greenish white, pink or blue, come in June and July and measure up to 20 centimeters across.

Chinese St. Johns Wort 金丝桃

(Hypericum chinense)

The Chinese Saint-John's-wort blossoms in summer, with flowers resembling those of a peach tree. Long, fine golden stamens stand out from the petals.

Distributed over China's central and southern provinces, this peach-like plant belongs to the temperate and warmer temperate zones. Growing one meter tall, the Saint-John's-wort flourishes beside rocks, at road corners, in lawns and in courtyards.

Medicines made from the root relieve fever and detoxify.

Part of the hypericum family, the Chinese Saint-John's-wort is an evergreen low shrub flowering in June and July. The sessile leaves are oval and opposite. The flowers are pale yellow and borne singly or in cymose clusters of three to seven flowers.

Cape Jasmine 栀子花

(Gardenia jasminoides)

The Cape jasmine is a popular garden and potted ornamental in southern China. Poet Du Fu extolled it 1,000 years ago: "Unlike other trees and flowers, the Cape jasmine is rare and precious on earth."

The glossy leaves are green year round, supporting snow-white flowers with a penetrating fragrance that lasts even when the blooms fade. For that reason, the flowers are often worn in corsages or kept in vases.

The Cape jasmine also has economic value. The root, leaves and fruit are known for their therapeutic effects, while the fruit can be utilized in yellow dyes and the flowers in perfumes.

The Cape jasmine is an evergreen shrub of the madder family, reaching three to four meters. It grows naturally along the Changjiang River and in southern and central China. It blossoms from June till August, each flower lasting about one month.

Chinese Trumpet Creeper   凌霄

(Campsis grandiflora)

The Chinese trumpet creeper has spread from the Changjiang River valley and the north to every part of the country.

Blossoming in summer and autumn, the tendrils of this ornamental vine cling to rocks, walls and trees. Showy flowers hanging from above sway in green leaves. The Chinese trumpet creeper climbs trellises to give shade form the scorching sun or to form decorative arches.

The flower, stem, leaves and root are fine madicinal ingredients.

A deciduous woody vine, the Chinese trumpet creeper is included in the bignonia family. The odd-numbered, veined, compound leaves are pointed ovals. The orange flowers arrive between June and September.

Arabian Jasmine 茉莉

(Jasminum sambac)

The tiny white flowers of the Arabian jasmine beam shyly in the night. Borne on new twigs, they display their purity from June to September before the first frost. Each flower lasts only 12-20 hours. The buds begin to open at dusk, climaxing between 9 and 10 o'clock at night.

The pungent aroma of the Arabian jasmine is as sweet as roses, as delicate as plums and as exquisite as orchids, pleasing both refined and simple noses. Poet Jiang Kui wrote, "When I write the history of flowers, the Arabian jasmine will be the first on my list."

Cultivation of the Arabian jasmine grew popular during the Han Dynasty (206 BC). The plant reached its heyday in the Song Dynasty (960 AD), when the emperor had several hundred pots of Arabian jasmine moved into his courtyards, filling the palace with fragrance. During the Ming Dynasty, essence from the Arabian jasmine was used in making face cream, while the Qing Dynasty brewed tea with dried jasmine flowers.

Belonging to the olive family, the Arabian jasmine is an evergreen shrub. The opposite leaves range from round to oval. White flowers carried on new branch tips appear in early June.

54

一九八〇年清明節
國亭作

Lotus 荷花

(Nelumbo nucifera)

The aquatic lotus is a favorite of the Chinese people. Green lotus leaves blanket the lakes in mid-summer, towered over by fresh flowers.

The lotus is a Chinese symbol of nobility and elegance. "Emerge from the mud unspoiled; washed by the ripples unseductive."

An ancient record says, "Emperor Zhao Di (60 A D) of the Han Dynasty planted lotuses in Lin Lake. This flowering plant was treasured by everyone in the palace."

Lotus flowers, opening in the morning in clear, bright colors and closing in the afternoon, release a pleasant fragrance. Walking by lotus ponds or boating through lotus flowers are relaxing on a hot summer day.

Lotus roots and seeds are edible. The leaves, stems, flowers, pods and roots are essential to Chinese medicine.

The lotus is a perennial aquatic herb. Its large, cylindrical root is white and fleshy. Shield-shaped leaves jut out of the water on long stalks. The single summer flowers are pink or white.

56

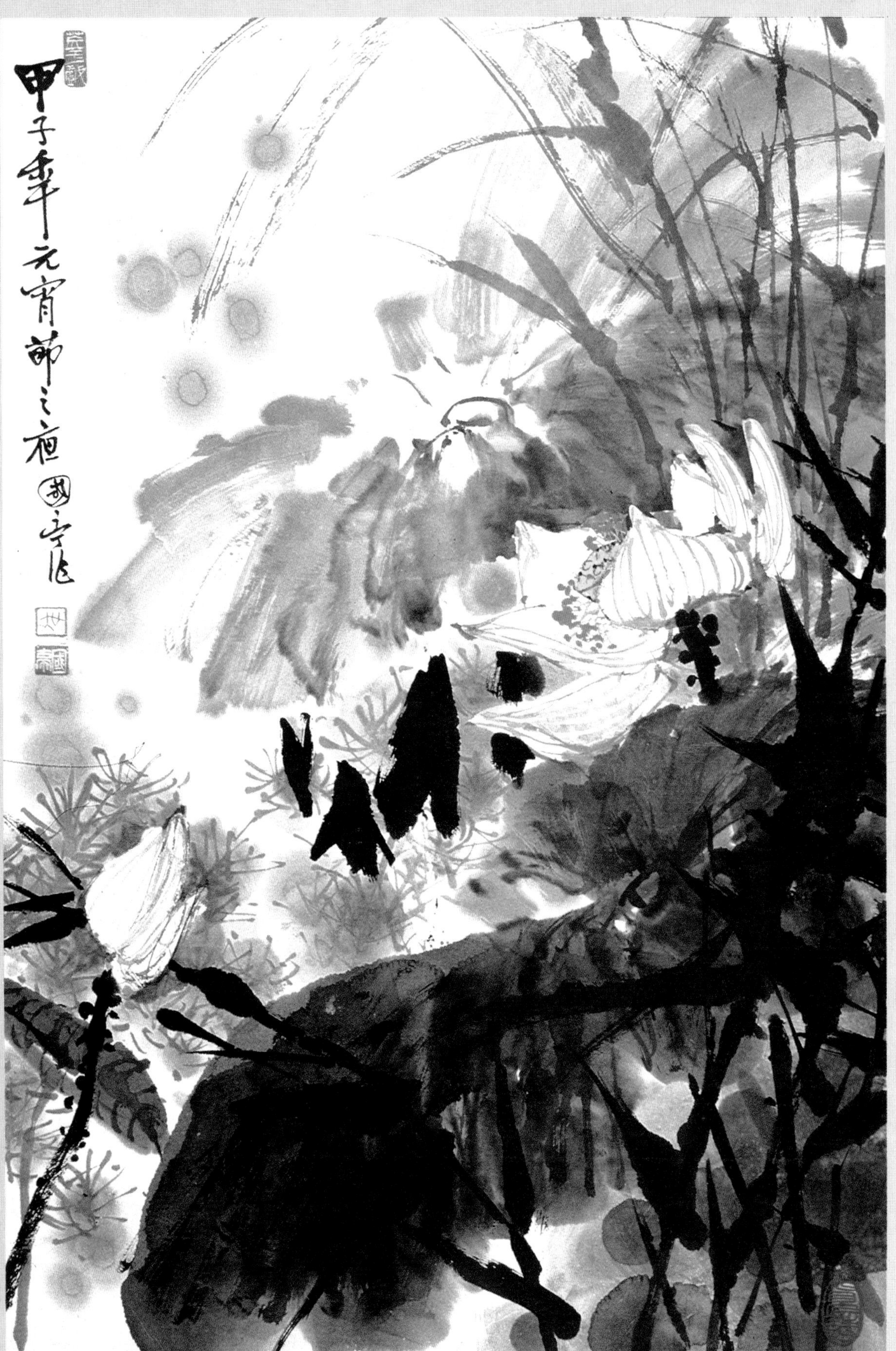
甲子年元宵節之夜

Tiger Lily 卷丹

(Lilium lancifolium)

The tiger lily originated in eastern and central China and is now planted all over the country. However, Jiangsu Province produces the best lilies, which have been raised in China for centuries for their edible and showy flowers.

The tiger lily likes sunshine and dry weather, but it tolerates cold winter days. Small clusters of blossoms, resembling tiny fluttering birds, open at mid-summer.

Planted together with perennial varieties, tiger lilies "bring a painted dragon to life" as the red tiger lily flowers sway in the breeze over a green carpet of creepers. The tiger lily can also be used to decorate forest glades.

The tiger lily, a bulb plant of the lily family, has lanceolate leaves. Coming in July, the drooping orange flowers have long filaments, with every three to six blooms arranged in racemose order.

Fragrant Plantain Lily 玉簪

(Hosta Plantaginea)

The fragrant plantain lily is an important ornament in classical Chinese gardens. Its Chinese name, *yu zan* (jade hairpin), describes the color and shape of its flower buds. Ancient Chinese women wore jade pins in their hair. Each dynasty featured distinctive hairstyles, and archaeologists can easily tell the period and social status of a woman by her coiffure.

Many Chinese poems mention elegant hairpins. Huang Tingjian of the Song Dynasty (960 AD) wrote: "A jade hairpin falls on the ground; no one comes to pick it up. Soon it changes into the most beautiful flower of South China."

The flowers of the fragrant plantain lily remind people of the elegant hair ornaments, so the plant became popular in China long ago, during the Han Dynasty (206 BC).

It grows along the Changjiang River, on the edges of woods and grassy slopes, and on the shady sides of rocks. Most beautiful in courtyards and flower beds, the plantain lily is also cultivated in potted landscapes.

Every part of the fragrant plantain lily is useful in making Chinese medicinal ointments which relieve swelling, inflammation and fever.

Of the lily family, the fragrant plantain lily is a stalkless herb. The leaves grow in clusters at the base of the plant. The fragrant white flowers bloom in July and August.

Rough Gentian   龙胆

(Gentiana scabra)

Although it is as famous in China as the azalea and the primrose, the rough gentian is not as widely cultivated. It grows wild on slopes, under bushes and at forest fringes, looking like ordinary grass. But when autumn comes, little bell-shaped flowers burst out, tinging the golden wilderness with bright violet.

The rough gentian originates in China, distributed from Heilongjiang, Jilin, Liaoning and Inner Mongolia down to Sichuan, Guizhou, Fujian, Guangxi and Guangdong. Medicines containing its root invigorate the stomach, relieve fever and dispel rheumatic pains.

Belonging to the gentian family, the rough gentian is a perennial herb with single, oval or lanceolate leaves opposite each other. The violet flowers are bell-shaped and the fruits oval. The rough gentian blossoms between August and September in central and north China, and between November and December in the south.

Short-Tube Lycoris 石蒜

(Lycoris radiata)

Originating in the Changjiang River valley and southwestern China, the short-tube lycoris grows in damp, shaded places on hillslopes, among grass or in rock crevices.

Its bright red flowers curve like dragon's claws, hence its Chinese name, *long zhua hua* (dragon's claw flower).

The short-tube lycoris lies dormant in summer without leaves and flowers. When autumn comes, its flower stalks shoot up from the ground. The flowers reach full bloom by September, but their stems begin to wither towards the end of the month, and leaves start to sprout. The leaves grow vigorously throughout the winter, and fall the following May, when the plant again enters its dormant stage.

The short-tube lycoris is often planted to border lawns and woods, in crevices of decorative rocks and in mixed perennial flower beds. People also arrange the cut flowers in vases.

The bulbs contain alkaloid, valuable for its medicinal properties.

The short-tube lycoris is a perennial, bulb herbal plant. The slender leaves grow at the base of the plant, while the red, funnel-shaped flowers appear in September in umbels.

Sweet Osmanthus　桂花

(Osmanthus fragrans)

The lustrous osmanthus flowers in the autumn, with shiny, fleshy foliage and grey bark.

Chinese people consider this evergreen tree princely, elegant and everlasting.

The sweet osmanthus has a strong scent that can travel far away on the air, reminding people of the rivers and mountains in their native land.

According to legend, an osmanthus tree stands in the lower right-hand corner of the moon. Giant Wu Gang tries to cut it down year after year, but the tree remains standing and thrives.

The sweet osmanthus is native to China's southwest and south-central regions, but is now adapted to all parts of the country.

The flowers are used to make tea, wine, medicine and perfume. The timber is good material for carving, while the bark is essential to dye-making.

The sweet osmanthus is an evergreen tree or shrub. The glossy oval leaves accent the pungently fragrant, yellowish white flowers.

66

Chrysanthemum   菊花

(Chrysanthemum morifolium)

Cultivation of the chrysanthemum began in China 3,000 years ago. Now a favorite ornamental flower, it was first regarded only as an edible and medicinal plant. The ancient medical treatise *Shennong Materia Medica* states that a dose of chrysanthemum gives you energy and puts spring in your steps. Ge Hong (284-364), a physician of the Eastern Jin Dynasty, described a chrysanthemum-covered valley in Henan Province, saying that the local people who drank from the river passing through the valley lived long lives.

The chrysanthemum likes sunshine, moisture and coolness, and tolerates cold weather. Over the centuries, 1,000 species, of different colors and shapes, have developed. All types bloom in mid-autumn when the temperature falls.

The chrysanthemum has been personified in many ways. Some people consider it haughty and unbending. Some sympathize with its loneliness and weakness. However, Tao Yuanming, the idyllic poet of the Eastern Jin Dynasty, was the first one to notice its splendor when he wrote, "The autumn chrysanthemum is such a beauty." Scholars of the following dynasties continued to value the chrysanthemum, and many new varieties appeared.

The chrysanthemum belongs to the composite family. The stem of this perennial herb, growing to 30-90 centimeters, is erect with many branches. The leaves, which are alternate, appear in many forms. The faintly fragrant flowers are borne at the top of the plant or at the axils in capitulum order. The size, color and shape of the flowers differ with various species.

甲子清明前の日國亭寫

Cotton Rose Hibiscus 木芙蓉

(Hibiscus mutabilis)

The cotton rose hibiscus, another name for the aquatic lotus, also refers to a terrestrial plant of the mallow family, which is extensively planted in Hunan and Sichuan provinces. Hunan is consequently known as the "kingdom of hibiscus," while Chengdu, capital of Sichuan, is called the "city of hibiscus."

The cotton rose hibiscus blossoms from mid-autumn to mid-winter, with large single or double-petal flowers. The flowers of the red hibiscus resemble those of the tree peony. The yellow hibiscus is a rare variety. The *san zui* hibiscus flowers change their colors several times a day, like a fairy changing her clothes. The *wen guan hua* hibiscus also changes colors.

Hardy, the hibiscus can be planted under walls, along roads, on slopes and at lakesides.

The bark provides good material for textile and paper-making industries. The flowers, leaves and root skins are ingredients in anti-inflammatory drugs.

Flowering between August and October, the cotton rose hibiscus, a member of the mallow family, is a deciduous shrub or low tree. It grows from two to five meters tall and has toothed, heart-shaped leaves. The single, semi-double or double-petaled flowers grow singly in red, white, and red and white.

Polyanthus Narcissus 水仙

(Narcissus tazetta var. Chinensis)

The polyanthus narcissus, in full bloom around the end of the year, nods gracefully over limpid waters and releases a delicate fragrance. Since ancient times, the narcissus has been known as the "riding-on-the-wave fairy."

In December, north China freezes under icy winds, but the blooming fresh narcissus creates springtime indoors.

The Chinese narcissus is native to the marshy lands along the southeastern coast in Zhejiang and Fujian provinces.

Zhangzhou in Fujian, known as the "home of narcissus," boasts special species that can be arranged in intricate patterns.

The polyanthus narcissus, of the amaryllis family, has egg-shaped bulbs covered with dark brown skin. The root is white, and the light green leaves are long and broad. The flower stalks, standing erect, bear four to eight white flowers between December and February.

Common Camellia 山茶

(Camellia japonica)

The ancient name for the camellia is the datura. It is also known as the *nai dong* (winter hardy). A favorite ornamental, it bursts into full bloom when winter begins. When it snows, the red flowers stand out against a sheet of white.

The camellia has been praised by many scholars. Poet Lu You of the Song Dynasty (960-1279) wrote, "It blossoms in the snow till spring; who can be more endurable to winter?"

Since ancient times, the camellia has been known for 10 prominent features: 1) It lives up to 400 years without aging; 2) It reaches a height of 50 feet; 3) The bark is rough, yet sleek; 4) The twigs intertwine into the shape of a dragon; 5) The roots curve in the form of grain bins; (6) The large leaves resemble tents; 7) It can tolerate snow and frost, and is green throughout the four seasons; 8) It flowers continuously for two to three months; 9) When kept in a vase, the flowers remain fresh for about two weeks; 10) It is attractive but not flashy.

Produced in east and central China, the common camellia decorates courtyards, garden paths, rocks and potted landscapes.

The wood is good carving material; the seeds can be pressed for oil; the leaves are essential in making soft drinks; and the flowers are medicinal ingredients.

The common camellia, an evergreen shrub, is of the tea family. The alternate leaves are in the shape of eggs. The faintly fragrant flowers are white, pink, red, rose or purple.

甲子年初春雨的日呈国中画求南京江苏省美术馆创作室

Winter Sweet 腊梅

(Chimonanthus praecox)

An ornamental that is unique to China, the winter sweet blossoms in winter, like the plum, when thousands of other flowers have withered and died. The winter sweet flowers are yellow and translucent like beeswax, and shaped like plum flowers, though the plants belong to two different families. In addition, the winter sweet's flowering period climaxes during the 12th moon of the lunar calendar, hence the Chinese name *la mei* (December plum).

Indigenons to central China, the winter sweet likes sunshine, tolerates shade and dampness, and endures cold. It now grows in all parts of China, especially in southern gardens, and looks best when arranged with bamboo. In the cold north, the winter sweet is displayed in vases.

The flowers can be used in preparing medicine and perfume.

A deciduous high shrub, the winter sweet can grow to three meters high. The leaves are oval and opposite. The subtly-fragrant flowers, borne singly on two sides of the twigs, bloom from December to March, after the leaves have fallen.

76

CATALOGUE

（京）新登字：**138号**

撰文：汪嘉熙、马悦

摄影：姜景余、严钟义、卢思聪、孟昭义、
　　　李承墉、张松泉、易　木、张景保、
　　　毛宗国

封面：王道中

责任编辑：王燕荣、于深泉

中国名贵花卉
（英文版）

吴国亭　绘画

出版者：**朝华出版社**
（中国国际图书贸易总公司出版机构）
中国北京车公庄西路**35号**　邮政编码：**100044**
印刷者：北京强华印刷厂
发行者：中国国际图书贸易总公司
中国北京车公庄西路**35号**　邮政编码：**100044**

中国北京第399号信箱
1986年第一版　1988年第二次印刷
1995年第三次印刷
84E － 635　04800

ISBN 7-5054-0418-0/J·0138